M000249619

From Lizzy's Lips to God's Ears

Waynette R. Cox

ISBN 978-1-0980-6833-2 (paperback)
ISBN 978-1-0980-6834-9 (digital)

Copyright © 2021 by Waynette R. Cox

All rights reserved. No part of this publication may be reproduced, distributed, or transmitted in any form or by any means, including photocopying, recording, or other electronic or mechanical methods without the prior written permission of the publisher. For permission requests, solicit the publisher via the address below.

Christian Faith Publishing, Inc.
832 Park Avenue
Meadville, PA 16335
www.christianfaithpublishing.com

Printed in the United States of America

I only wanted to send a special thank you and acknowledgements to a young lady that helped me create my characters her name is (Aniyah McGibbney).

Introduction

Hello, allow me to introduce myself to you. My name is Alexandra Elizabeth Sullivan. My family calls me Lil Lizzy, in case you are wondering. Yes, both names have been passed down to me through my grandmothers, whom I love with all my heart. We live right outside of New York City, not directly in the city; but if we need to go, we are literally five minutes away.

My neighborhood block is very friendly, and everyone loves one another. I live with my parents, Mr. and Mrs. Sullivan, our neighbors refer to them as Ricky and Afiya, but I am only expected to address them as Mom and Dad, which is what I should be doing anyway! Our house sits in the middle of the block. It's a clean, quiet block, but sometimes it can get very noisy, especially when we have our block parties, I'll tell you guys more about them later.

Chapter 1

Just let tell you about all my friends, Yung-Su, who is Asian, thinks he's a rap artist! Now, don't get me wrong, anyone can do or be anything that they chose; however, he just looks so funny when he tries to dress like he is from Roc-A-Fella. His eyes are slanted, and his face is slightly round, and he's really kind short. But he thinks he is a hip-hop artist, for real. His parents let him go see one Jay-Z concert, and his life has not been the same. That kid is one funny dude; he even dresses like a hip-hop artist—hat turned to the back, pants sagging—and I'll be like, "Boy, pull your pants up! We don't want to see your underwear!" He just nods his head and laughs.

And then there's Malcolm. Now I think I got a crush on Malcolm for real. Malcolm is very tall for a twelve-year-old boy. He has dark brown skin, which is very smooth, and nice, wavy hair. Malcolm always looks nice too. His sneakers are clean, his shorts are clean, and so are his white T-shirts. His mother always make sure he looks nice all the time. Malcolm is also on the baseball team, so we go to the park to watch him play. He's an outfielder, so we talk a lot of trash while he's out there!

Now Justina, that's my homegirl. We are very tight, and we're always together. Sometimes people are less fortunate, so my mom lets me give Justina some of my clothes. I never say anything because I don't want to embarrass her at school.

Nevertheless, I love her so much because she's always there for me. At night, when I'm praying, I always say a special prayer for Justina and her annoying brother, Shoobie. By the way, Shoobie has Down syndrome. In case you have never seen someone with Down syndrome, their facial features are different from others. Shoobie has very small eyes and a small nose, and he has a small body stature. Kids used to bully him, but we all pitched in and stopped it. And now he lives a normal life where people don't tease him—at least, in our neighborhood!

I asked God, "Why did he make him that way?" I learned that it's because we're all different, but he loves us all just the same; and although we may be different, we're still very much alike! What I mean by that is, we all experience the same emotions—we all cry, we all laugh, and we all can do most of the same things. However, some people are better at doing things than others! The bottom line is, I pray to God every day, all day, because he listens to me and I know that he is up there in that big, blue sky watching over me and my whole family and your whole family too! When I see the birds flying, I see the sun up in the sky, I see the trees blowing, the grass is green—oh, I know that we have a Creator. I don't know about you, but I know we have one.

By the way, school's out for the summer, and it's going to be a blast! We have so many fun things that we can do. Most of the time, we like it when the fire department opens up the water plug; but today, I think Malcolm has a baseball game, so we'll all be headed to the park this afternoon to watch him play. That's probably later on after we go get our ice water and just walk around our neighborhood like we normally do; after all, we have the whole summer to look forward to.

We also have to check on our older neighbors so that they have water and things that they need from the store because that's part of our daily job—to make sure that we do the daily runs for them. Like I said, our block is very, very close, and we protect each other. We do have a diverse our neighborhood. Did I mention Yung-Su's parents own a dry cleaner down the street? So that helps our community.

Then there is Mr. Thomas who owns our local grocery store. He has good penny candy and the best snow cones *ever*! He will also let other people open tabs until their payday if they are low on food or whatever they may need. I thank God for him because he helps a lot of people, especially Justina's parents. Don't mention this, but I know that Justina's parents are having a rough time right now, and they can sure use the help! So remember, folks, God is good in my book! Always pray for others—you never know when you will need someone.

"Hey, guys, we are heading there, let's go!"

That's Malcolm yelling down the street, so we better get moving as quickly as possible or he won't stop yelling. He just gets so excited when he goes near a baseball field. (I wish you guys could hear how loud he is right now.) It don't make no sense! Lol.

Justina and I sit with Yung-Su and watch Malcolm and his team win the baseball game by a landslide. Yung-Su spots a man with the monkey, and we just can't leave the park without some real laughter. Anyway, Mr. Malcolm decides he wants to see the monkey do some tricks. He asks the man if the monkey can do anything interesting.

"Sure can," the man replies. "What would you like to see him do?"

"Anything, 'cause I don't think he can!"

"Gotta quarter?"

"Yep! Right here," Malcolm says, handing the man the quarter.

The man pulls out a red ball and throws the ball high in the sky. When the ball hit the ground, the monkey takes off after the ball and runs back to the man.

"Anybody could do that!" Malcolm says.

That's when the man tells the monkey, "Give it to him, I mean *give* it to him!"

The monkey tosses the ball right at Malcolm's head and clumps him something good!

"Are you okay?" the man asks Malcolm. "Was that a good enough trick for you, young man? Here's your quarter back. I won't let the monkey charge you today!"

We all literally could not stop laughing. It was the funniest thing *ever*!

On our way home, we always take the long way back, but for some reason, the Spirit told me to walk home quickly. I don't know how I managed to convince the others to walk along with me, but they did, and guess what? As we approach our block, we hear sirens, and now we see flashing lights! Oh my gosh! What's happening on our block?

We all take off running, only to discover there's a kid on the ground and a mangled bicycle lying in the road. People are moving quickly back and forth, and now the police have roped off the immediate area.

"Who's the kid on the ground that the paramedics are working on?" everyone is asking.

We all start to look around to see which one of us is missing. Almost in slow motion, all at the same time, we yell, "Shoobie! Oh my god, it's Shoobie on the ground!"

Stanley Edward "Shoobie" Green surely has been a pain in everyone's backside, as my grandma says. But he's *our* Shoobie, and we love him dearly. Everyone's parents are now scurrying around the neighborhood doing their head count of their own children. So what happened to him? His friends say that Shoobie was horseplaying as usual on his bike, in and out between cars, not paying attention; but when they looked up, it was too late. The driver never even saw him in front of his car. Shoobie ended up on the ground., not moving at *all*!

Justina is totally hysterical. I'm trying to console her, but it's not easy because she is crying, and pulling away, and trying to go toward the ambulance; and we are trying to stop her from going in the street.

Please, God, help me help my friend, I think. *She needs me right now!*

As the ambulance pulls away, Justina begins calming down and wiping her tears away. Justina's mom asks if she could stay with my family that evening, and of course, it's not a problem. After all, we are concerned that Shoobie is going to be fine. That's when it hit me! I will start a prayer vigil on our block for Shoobie. If I can get the whole block to talk to God with me, then Shoobie will be fine! 'Cause, see, that's how he works—the more people that pray and believe in him, the more the miracles he can do!

That night was very quiet in my house; although we sit every evening and have family time over our dinner, this night was truly different. No one is saying much; we just pick over our food and kinda make no eye contact with each other. My parents are pretty cool people, always laughing and teasing, but not tonight! I really need to pray about the prayer vigil for Shoobie because I hope everyone believes in God like I do.

*****

The next morning, after saying my morning prayers and giving my thanks to God, I go straight into making the vigil happen. Justina is up and ready to go check on her brother, so I think my mom who is also a nurse will take us to the hospital (at least, I hope, if she lets me go as well). I overheard my mom talking to Justina's mom, and she asks her to bring Justina and come right away. So off we go to the trauma center 'cause Shoobie might be in pretty bad shape.

Sure enough, poor Shoobie is not breathing on his own. He has suffered a concussion, a broken arm, and a broken leg too!

Oh my, what was he doing on his bike? I think. *Now, we all can agree that he is a real pain in the* you know what! *But please, God, let our little brother pull through. He's a really special kid in my book, and he deserves to have another chance, God.*

Shoobie has tubes coming out of his nose and all kinds of other tubes going inside him that I can't see from where I was, but that's enough for me anyway. I think all the excitement and the nurses and doctors running around are a bit much for us all, so the grown-ups feel it best if we all go home for the time being, which was cool with me 'cause that gives me time to do what I need to do.

The whole block was buzzing with the Shoobie stories. I even hear an old lady from down the block say that Shoobie is dead! Ms. Lady, you don't know what you're talking about. We just literally left the hospital, and no, Shoobie is not dead! But because my parents are raising me to respect my elders, I refused to correct her, to save myself from getting in trouble. I just keep walking until I catch up with Malcolm and Yung Jay-Z—oops, I meant Yung-Su! He would be beaming from ear to ear if he knew I called him Jay-Z!

As Justina and I finally find the two, they are arguing about basketball teams and whose team is better!

"Hey, guys, I plan on starting a prayer vigil on our block tomorrow evening for Shoobie," I say. "Can I count on my friends to support me?"

"Sure, but what's a prayer vigil?" asks Malcolm.

"It's when people come together with candles, and they pray for whoever is in need of prayer and comfort for the grieving family."

"Lizzy, how do you even know all this grown-up stuff?"

"My grandma Lizzy told me all about praying and talking to God when I was much younger. Yes, I know I'm only twelve but, she taught me to trust him and to have a relationship with him."

"So how do you know he even exists?" Yung-Su wants to know. "You can't see him!"

"I know, but he is with us. Watch how fast Shoobie is going to come home!"

"Yung-Su, ain't nobody worried about you," Malcom teases. "Take your little fake hip-hop wannabe self on somewhere!"

Everyone is laughing now, and he is trying to act like he is angry.

"Where you going?" Malcom says. "I was just playing wit ya! Can't take a joke then, oh well!"

"He always sounding off on me, and I don't be saying nothing!" Yung-Su says, leaving the group.

I guess Malcolm is going to his house, so Justina and I decide to sit on my stoop and just take in the warm summer air and look up at the stars. Things have now calmed down, and our block is back to normal. It looks like the stars are falling out the sky on us. This is a beautiful night, and even with all the drama that happened earlier today, it's still a peaceful night.

"Good night, good Morning, world! We made it to a new day," my grandma used to say.

My grandma said that I should learn to do one good deed a day and then I will be blessed. So my good deed will be going to our local library to print out some fliers for my prayer vigil. My dad is the bomb 'cause all he ever says is, "Sure, Lizzy baby, whatever you like!" He likes to drive me and my friends around, so off to the library we go. But please don't tell my mom that we talked my dad into stopping us by the mall for cute new earrings! He brought Justina some as well. So I'ma be thinking I am cute when Malcolm sees these earrings.

As soon as we pull up to our house, Justina's mom and dad are waiting for us. They still look very sad, so Shoobie may be the same. My dad hugs them both, and they head into our house.

"Daddy, can I walk around and hand out my fliers?" I ask him.

"Sure, Lizzy baby, but as soon as you are done, please come straight home!"

"Yes, Daddy, I will."

"Keep your cell phone on," he reminds me.

"Yes, Daddy!"

Handing out my fliers and talking to people make me realize that maybe *everyone* doesn't believe in God. Some people farther down my block crumpled up their flier and threw it away right in my face! But that's not going to stop me. I'm on a mission for Shoobie! That's all I know.

After handing out the last of the fliers, I ask my parents if we could maybe have like a small cookout to feed our neighbors and then maybe we can get them to come out and pray with us. When I tell you my parents are super supportive of this, they waste no time saying *yes*—they're in! And just like that, we are having a block party for Shoobie! Mr. Thomas agreed to donate snow cones for the block, so yes, this is going to be all right. Justina's mom makes the best potato salad, so she is making that; and my dad loves to grill, so he got the burgers and hotdogs.

On the day of the vigil, I was really nervous! So why did I pray if I am this nervous, you ask? I sure don't know cause my Grandma Lizzy says, "If you pray, don't worry 'cause if you worry, you don't need to waste your time praying." That's a good one. I can't wait to go and visit her. I know right now would not be a good time because Justina and Shoobie need us here.

As everyone is starting to gather outside our stoop, my father got that grill smoking. Malcolm brought his boom box and he is playing music, Yung-Su is rapping on the mic, and the whole neighborhood is cracking up laughing at the crazy boy. I think he looks hilarious! My father asked Justina's dad, Mr. David, to lead us in praying over the food; and as he is praying, it seems like I can feel God standing right on our block with all of us.

"Let's eat" is all we heard Mr. Thomas say, and everyone burst out with laughter!

My parents are passing out food along with Ms. Yvette (Justina's mom) and Ms. Gloria (Malcolm's mom) also helping. Ms. Kim, Yung-Su's mom, made her famous egg rolls everyone on the block loves them things. They are always the first to go. As I watch everyone laughing and enjoying this affair, I don't want anyone to forget why we are having this in the first place. So I take the mic from Yung-Su, and I begin to ask everyone to come close together.

"Excuse me, but can I have everyone's attention? Please?" I say. "Thank you for participating and for supporting this function for our Shoobie and his family. I just feel really bad for my best friend and what happened to her little brother, so I asked myself what I could do to make them feel better, and you all came through in a big way! I am proud to live on Franklin Street, and I hope we never have to leave here because I don't know what I would do without having support and love like this from so many people. So can everyone bow their heads? Oops! Mom, we forgot to give everyone a candle to hold up for Shoobie."

"I got you Lizzy," I hear Malcolm say.

That's why I have that secret crush 'cause he always is there to pick up the slack!

And as everyone bows their heads, I begin to ask God to lift up Shoobie in the name of Jesus, just like my grandma told me to! I don't know about anyone else, but I felt a jolt in the bottom of my stomach. That was the spirit of my grandpa Ricky Sr. say "Lizzy baby" from heaven. He's my dad's father, and he passed away and he's in heaven. I sure do miss him too!

"*Shoobie will come home, and he will be fine!*" I hear God say.

The good thing about this vigil is that someone started a bucket, and people are putting money in for Justina's family. How awesome is that? No one had to even asked! Now that's what you would call a village! I am so excited about this because for once, since this whole thing happened, my friend and her parents are smiling!

Hey, wait a minute, is that the man and the monkey from the park? I think. *Oh no, where's Malcolm 'cause I know he is sick of that monkey!*

Well, for now, the monkey is close by the man, so I think there might be too many people for him because he hopped on the man's shoulder. He's scared but not too scared to hop down from the man's shoulder to dance. This monkey is too much for me. He heard the music and lost his monkey mind! Lol.

As the day winds down and things start to slow down, Justina's parents thank me and everyone who helped out, which happens to be everyone. We all assure them that they would have done the same for us. That's how my parents are helping me to grow and be responsible in helping who I can along my journey in life so that I may get help when and if I need it. Makes sense to me 'cause sometimes your parents don't make a bit of sense. I am very tired so I end my day by thanking everyone, kissing my parents good night, and sleeping really tight.

*****

All I remember is my alarm clock screaming "Lil Lizzy, get up!" Don't ask me why my father decided to set my clock to say that, but he thinks it's the funniest thing ever. I don't! The sun is so bright, and the birds are in full effect at my window! Wow, good morning! Now I can smell bacon and I hear my father talking loudly to my mother, so I need to do an investigation of my own.

"What's up, Daddy? Why are you yelling?"

"Nothing, Lizzy baby, just talking to your mom about Aunty Faye."

Now, Aunty Faye is my dad's younger sister. She is a freelancer—whatever my father means, I have yet to understand. I just don't question my father when he appears to be upset, and this is that time. Instead of not listening to him and pushing for an answer, I decide to go get dressed for the day and let him tell me later.

"*Good choice, Lizzy baby!*" It was my grandpa again!

Yung-Su and Malcolm are heading back to the park, but I am staying close to home, just in case I hear some good news about Aunty Faye and Shoobie.

My mom worked on the same unit that Shoobie was on, so that made everyone—especially Justina's parents—feel better knowing that a whole other set of eyes are watching over him. Shoobie hasn't opened his eyes yet, but God did tell me it wouldn't be too much longer before he does. And I know that we all will be so happy when he finally wakes his annoying self up. I would rather have him getting on my last nerves than be lying up there in the hospital in a semicoma. That means that he has little brain activity. (See, that's why we should learn to listen to our parents.) My mom told me about the cause of the brain activity, but I am sure you guys are probably thinking how I know all of that.

So now the doctors are just waiting to see what's going to happen from here. In the meantime, I need to find out exactly what that phone call from Grandma Lizzy was all about! I got brushed off last night, but not today! I need answers 'cause my daddy was very upset, and my father don't let nothing get to him. People say I'm like my daddy—laid back! Now, my mama, she is no joke! She's very loving and very kind, but don't cross her *please*! They are too quiet, so that's the red flag. Usually they are teasing each other, but today nothing of the sort is happening right now. Maybe it's because of Shoobie? No, 'cause they were fine before the phone call from my Grandma Lizzy.

I wonder what she said to my dad to upset him so terrible? I think. *If I call my grandma and ask her, that may disappoint my parents for going behind them or should I wait? What would you do? What would Jesus do? I think I need to stay in a young child's place and wait for my parents to let me in on the big secret! That's the safest thing I can come up with right now.*

It's not that I am afraid of my mother and father; I just know to respect them, *no matter what*! Hey, kids out there, you got that? Honor your mother and your father given to you from God! I may come off as a "grown" little kid, but I am *well* trained, and I listen to the sound of my parents' voice—what I mean is, when they speak, I listen! As my parents, they have nothing but positive energy for me, and I thank God I am smart enough to receive what has been given to me!

I now have the courage to ask my dad since he appears to have calmed down some.

"Daddy, what did Grandma Lizzy say to upset you so bad last night?"

"Lizzy baby, come here and sit down. I need to talk to you, and I wanted your mom to be here, but she is working late with Shoobie tonight, so it's me and you, kid."

He calls me kid when he hates to have to tell me something.

"There is no easy way to tell you this, but we may need to move to Georgia with Grandma Lizzy," Daddy tells me.

"What! No way, Daddy! This can't be happening right now!" I protest. "My best friend needs me right now, and all you guys can think about is moving? Whose idea is this and why?"

"Now, listen to me. You need to pull your whole attitude in right now, Lizzy baby! You acting like you the only one that is going to be affected! None of *us* thought about this."

"Why can't she move here to New York with us, Daddy? I don't want to go!"

"I am sure you don't, and guess what? Me either! Okay, just think about this, Lizzy baby. If something were to happen to your grandmother, my mother and I could not live with ourselves. So we have to do what's right by her, Lizzy. I promise it won't be all bad. You will meet new friends and start a new school."

As the tears fall from my eyes, I can only help but think about Justina and Shoobie, and Yung-Su, and, oh my god, Malcolm!

"No, Daddy, we just can't go! She has to move here, please, Daddy, I really don't want to go!"

"Lizzy baby, calm down, we are not leaving today or next week! But soon, okay? You have plenty of time."

"What happened to Aunty Faye? Where is she? And why did she leave? That's a darn shame!"

"Hey, young lady, watch your mouth!" my daddy says. "Lizzy, we need to talk later when you calm down 'cause right now, you're barking up the wrong tree!"

Oops, he is mad! I say to myself.

"Sorry. Daddy! It's just that—"

"Nope, Alexandra Elizabeth Sullivan, later!"

That's it—I'm on the stoop for now. Outside the sun is warm and the stoop is hot to sit on, but I am so upset right now, I can't think straight. Although it is hot, I just want to think about something else.

Sorry, Grandma Lizzy, it's not that I don't love you, it's just that my life is here! I think. *And what about Shoobie and the others on this block who love Ricky and Afiya Sullivan? They can't act like they won't be hurt 'cause they will be.*

Anyway, Justina and her dad are pulling up and coming home from the hospital.

"Hey, Mr. David. Hey, Justina, you coming back out?"

"Who said I was going in, knucklehead?" Justina tells me.

"Don't get smart with me, girlfriend, I got you!" I tell her.

We go back and forth all day long; it's our way of saying "what's up?"

"How's Shoobie?" I ask Justina.

"He still hasn't opened his eyes, but he's breathing on his own now. The doctor told my parents that he is out of the woods, whatever that means."

"He's going to be fine, knucklehead!"

We both giggle and laugh loudly. I give Justina a shrug on her arm to let her know it's okay. That's why she's my best friend because we can act like this with each other and still love each other. She don't get mad at me, and I don't pay her any mind! Speaking of which, I need to tell her but how? And where do I start?

Okay, just calm down, Lizzy baby, and just tell her! I think.

"Okay," I say out loud.

"Okay what?" Justina asks.

Oops! I said okay out loud, and Justina heard me!

"Umm, okay, I gotta tell you a secret."

"What is it? Just slow down, Queen Quicky!" Justina says back.

"Queen who?" I joke to her. "Anyway, my Grandma Lizzy in Georgia is now living alone, and she needs—"

"Wait, don't say it, Lizzy!"

"Yes, girl, we moving to Georgia!"

"No way! What about us?"

"That's what's I said! I asked the same question."

"And what did they say, Lizzy?"

"My father is completely upset, not 'cause he don't love his mama but that we have to pack up and leave our life here and start a new life there. He said new school, new friends."

"New Friends? Heck no! We are your friends! You said you never wanted to leave here, you just said it, Lizzy, you told the whole neighborhood!"

"I know, Justina! You don't need to keep reminding me, do you? Well..."

"Well what?"

"I'm going in the house to lay down. I have a headache, the sun is hot, and I don't feel so good. See ya later."

"Okay, Lizzy, feel better.

"Thanks," I tell Justina as I head into the house.

Heading up to my room, my dad is on the phone again. This time, it's my Aunty Faye, but I have no energy to be nosy because I need to rest my head. Thinking about everything has made me nauseous.

*****

I must have been asleep for a while 'cause I'm starting to smell my mom's famous Jamaican ribs and rice and beans! Yes, I'm smelling exactly what I smell!

"Hey, Momma," I say to her.

"Hey, baby gurl, how ya holding up, mon?"

"Well, Daddy told me about the phone call."

"I know, sweetie. You just have to adjust somehow. Neither your father nor myself wants to leave New York! But, baby gurl, what's Momma Lizzy supposed to do?"

"It ain't fair!" I complain.

"Hey, ya mouth going to getcha somting, mon! Watch out!"

Well, our conversation is not going to get any better, so I offer to help in the kitchen.

"Set the table, Lizzy, please and thank ya, mon!"

"Your welcome, Mom!"

I smile 'cause somehow, God just told me, "*You're going to be fine, Lizzy,*" and that's where I am going to leave it for now.

During dinner, my mother received a call that Shoobie opened his eyes. Yes, go, Shoobie! We are up jumping up and down, and suddenly the move to Georgia doesn't matter! Shoobie is *awake*! Special thanks to you, God, 'cause you're making all this possible! We all run out the house next door to Justina's house, and they too are already in the street jumping up and down, and people are screaming and some are laughing and crying. I am looking up in the sky right now 'cause, God, you really do *love* every one of *us*!

"Shoobie is awake, can we go and see him? Please, can we?" I ask my mom.

"Yes, but the doctors don't want him to get too excited, so not right now. But maybe later."

"Yeah!"

"Hey, I'm calling Malcolm and Yung-Su to tell them," I tell Justina.

"I bet you are!"

"Be quiet, Justina, you always in somebody's business! You too young to have business! Anyway, Malcolm, where y'all at? Okay. Well, guess what? Yes, my hair is still nappy, smarty-pants! Anyhoo, Shoobie is awake! Yes, he is! We just got the phone call from the hospital, and everyone is on the block right now celebrating. Y'all coming down here? Okay, see you in a few, boy!"

"Look at you all cheesed up over that boy! Do Ricky and Afiya know you all head over heels for Malcolm?"

"Stop it, Justina, and I'm not playing with you!"

"Okay, okay. I'm done. But seriously, did you tell him yet that you guys are leaving?"

"No, I didn't get a chance too. I will tell him later, I don't want to spoil the happiness for Shoobie. It will only make it worse, so I'm going to tell him on my own. Hey, big-mouth Justina, I'm *going* to *tell* him *myself!*"

"Okay!"

"Please let me tell him?" I beg Justina.

"Okay, okay, okay! Look at Yung-Su, he is ridiculous! But you got to love his style. For an Asian kid, he got it going on!"

"Uh-oh, Justina is liking herself some Yung-Su!"

"Friends, girl, and that's it! We are twelve years old, girl, what's wrong with you?"

"Well, we are going to high school next year, and that's when it all starts."

"What all starts, Justina?"

"Ask your mom."

"No 'stank' you very much, don't feel like getting my face slapped today!"

"Sike!"

"My parents assured me that we would be having this conversation before school starts again, so I think I'll wait until then, plus I got good sense!"

"You don't want to know about the birds and bees?" Justina teases.

"What? Girl, stop talking for now, please. I just can't with you right now!"

"Oh, okay, I get it. You scared?"

"Scared of what, Justina? Am I missing something here?"

"Um, yes!"

"Well, just the same, Justina. I think I want to wait for my parents to have the talk with me, if that's okay with you?"

We laugh and giggle again.

Once Yung-Su and Malcolm show up, we all start to horseplay and play tag with each other, and just staying loose to the block is what I'm trying to do these days.

"God, do you think I talk too much? I don't know where that came from, but do you, God?" I tell God. "If I don't talk to you all the time, I won't know what to do next. You keep me going, and my grandma said, 'Don't ever get too proud or you can't call on the Lord!' I know people probably say I'm too grown, but who cares what they say because I'm a child of God, no matter what! My parents taught me well is all."

Chapter 2

I hear the adults talking about Shoobie coming home in a couple of weeks, wow! The summer will almost be over, and we will be back to school. Oops! I won't be, but they will! I'm just happy that he is all right. He broke his arm and his leg, so he's going to need plenty of help. That's what I should be thinking about anyway and not my own problems.

"Hey, you guys, what can we do for Shoobie when he gets home? I think we need to have another block party?"

"Hey, that would be the bomb!" says Malcolm.

"We can ask for the neighborhood to pitch in again," Justina adds. "And we can sweep up the sidewalks for extra money to help pay for a new bike for Shoobie. Lizzy baby, you are so awesome! You always think about other people before yourself."

"That's why she my girl," Malcolm jokes.

"Oh," Justina starts to tease.

"Justina, there you go again, girl! So who's in?"

"We all in, Lizzy, quit playin' girl," Yung-Su says.

"Cool, let's get this ball rolling!"

As we decide who will sweep and who will pick up paper, I see the grown-ups in a circle talking, and now my curiosity has gotten the best of me so I try to slip off to be in earshot of their conversation 'cause I'm nosey. Guess who sent me back down the street with the rest of the kids? My mother. Boom!

Just like that, she says, "Go on back down there with your friends...adults are talking!"

"Well, we have our own stuff to do anyway!" I say.

Ms. Gloria called Justina to tell her that they would be going to the hospital this afternoon, so she needed to stay close to home. I wonder if my parents will let me go. As I was about to ask, my father looked at me and nodded his head; he already knew what I was about to say! How does he do that?

After making our block spotless, we collected our money and put it in our friends' bank that we share. Malcolm's mom lets us keep it at their house, and we also made enough to get Shoobie a nice bike. If we don't have enough, my dad will put the rest of the money to it! Ain't that nice of him? Told y'all my dad is the man! And ain't *ain't* a word I'm told.

As we all fill up our cars and head to the hospital, I say my special prayer, praying that Shoobie will be happy to see us all. And sure enough, Shoobie is sitting up eating ice cream and watching cartoons. He is so happy to see us all, he starts to cry.

"Don't cry, Shoobie, it's okay," Justina says.

"We love you too, Shoobie!" all the others add.

After all the commotion is over and everyone calms down, we all sign his casts. He has a broken arm and leg, so we could sign anywhere we choose! Of course, Yung-Su can draw, so he is making a robot so Shoobie can see it every day! It's pretty cool looking so, we won't get on him too bad this time!

God, how quickly you opened up Shoobie's eyes and now he's up eating ice cream—it's a real miracle that we are all looking at right now! Everyone is talking at the same time, and you can't even hear the nurse coming in to check on Shoobie's vital signs.

"Excuse me please," Nurse Nancy announces. "Could I have everyone leave the room for just a moment so that I may check on this young man? Who, by the way, is a miracle right now in front of us. Thank you all very much, and I will be out of your way shortly."

As we all file out of his room into the hallway, we are quickly reminded that we're in a hospital and our noise level is way too loud. Oops! Even the adults are embarrassed!

So as we head to the cafeteria to grab a bite to eat, walking the halls and seeing all the sick people make me feel bad for them. With each room that I pass, I say a silent prayer for each person in a room in a hospital bed that they get well again. There, I feel better already! Eating pizza and talking as a group is bringing us all closer, and it's unfortunate why we are here but at least we are together.

"Shoobie likes clowns," I say to Dad. "Can we get him a clown when he comes home from the hospital?"

"We shall see," my father is quick to answer me, in case someone else said no.

That's how he is about his Lizzy baby—the first to stand up for his baby girl! That's a better possibility than just a straight no! So I'll take that for now, but you can count on it that I'm getting that clown for Shoobie!

Leaving the hospital, we all were very tired. It has been a long day, and so we say our goodbyes for the evening and we go our separate ways. Our car ride home is quiet once again; no one says anything. I guess there's nothing to say right now, so sometimes you just gotta ride with the silence. I'm wondering if I should mention to my mom about the whole "Aunty Faye and Grandma Lizzy" stuff or should I just keep quiet? I think I will just relax for now. It has been too much on my dome for one day!

By the way, my dad calls my head a dome. I'm taking it as a big head? What ya think? One thing my dad does is always makes me and my mom laugh 'cause he is super funny. Ricky Sullivan—he swears he's funny like "comedian funny," but my mom and I always tell him to keep his day job.

As much as I want to have a discussion, I refused 'cause my eyelids are so heavy. It feels like someone is standing on them! Good night, all!

*****

My phone is ringing off the hook, and I know it can only be one person, Justina. And sure enough, it's her!

"Girl, what do you want?" I say first.

"Malcolm is going to ask you to be his girlfriend!"

"Huh, what did you just say, Big Mouth?"

"You heard me, Lizzy baby! Malcolm wants you to go out with him. I mean, you cute and he cute, y'all look cute together."

"So he waiting for me to click over and give him an answer?"

"What should I tell him?"

"Look, Big Mouth, just tell him to call me so I can tell him about Georgia."

"Oh, um, about Georgia he already knows!" Justina tells me now.

"What! You are sickening, Justina! How could you betray me like that! I thought we are supposed to be like sisters? I am supposed to tell Malcolm, not you!"

"We are sisters, and we share everything! Your news is my news, my news is your news!" she tells me.

"Oh, heck no! You have crossed the line, and I am not feeling your negative energy right now, so catch me later!"

"See you!"

"No see, *you*!"

Justina has really done it this time. I love her, but right now she is done in my book. What do I mean "done"? So here's Malcolm beeping in, and I am thinking about what to do.

"Hey, Malcolm, what's up?"

"Did you talk to Justina?" he asks.

"You mean Big Mouth?"

"Yo, Lizzy, chill. What's going on with you?"

"I'll tell you what's going on! We gotta move to Georgia cause my dumbass aunty left my grandma alone."

"Lizzy, watch your language!"

"Well, it's the truth. I love her and all, but right now, she is getting on my last available nerve. It's taking everything in me to not give her a phone call!"

"Or what? You gonna call her and say what? Lizzy, you got to get a hold of yourself and think about what you got going on right now. We need to focus on Shoobie getting out of the hospital. And what about Justina? What did she that was so bad that you're not talking?"

"First off, Malcolm, don't act like that with me. I told Justina that I wanted to tell you myself about Georgia! And what did her big mouth do? She ran her mouth! She shouldn't have said anything, but—"

"Why, Lizzy?"

"Because I like you, Malcolm! There, I said it. You happy now?"

"Oh, oh, okay! It's cool, Lizzy, 'cause today is your lucky day 'cause I dig you too!"

"Go somewhere, Malcolm! Now you think you all super cool and stuff! Don't be running around telling the whole block! I ain't playing with you either!"

So after telling Malcolm the truth about how I feel about him, it does somehow make me feel better. Now all I have to do is make up with Justina. I know she has a big mouth and can't hold water, but still, that's my home girl from daycare, and I can't let us slip away from each other. Although other people are not so nice to her at school, I took on the role of her protector from all the bullying, so she needs me too! So I'm going to call her right now.

"Hey, girl… I am so sorry for acting out on you in front of everyone, but you knew that I wanted to tell Malcolm myself."

"I'm sorry too, sister friend, cause one thing I do have is a big mouth! But I promise from this day forward, I will keep all your secrets. Kool?"

"Kool!"

"How you making out with Shoobie's coming-home block party?" she asks me.

"Well, girl, so far, we made enough money to replace his bike with a brand-new one, and my dad said if we need more money, he would pitch in."

"You guys are awesome! Should I tell my parents?"

"There you go again! I don't care if you tell them, Justina, 'cause you going to anyway!"

We laugh and giggle together.

You know what, God, I am so glad that I have a personal relationship with you 'cause sometimes some of your creations get on my nerves! I can't help it, God, but they do! But if I stay focused on Shoobie, this move to Georgia, my crush on Malcolm, and Justina's big mouth won't really matter right now.

So going over my list, and it looks like things will come together again. I sure pray that Shoobie pays attention to the cars when he's on his new bike. I certainly would not want him to repeat this and have another terrible accident.

Oh shoot, one of my favorite shows is about to come on, *Dish Nation*. I love them, especially the Da Brat, and it's only that I will soon be turning thirteen that I can watch the show 'cause "Ricky" and "Afiya" had to watch the show first to see if I would be permitted watch. Sometimes, they go overboard, but hey, kids gonna get it from somewhere! My mom says that parents need to teach their children at home first, and then when we go out into the world, we know right from wrong.

What is Yung-Su on my phone? I wonder. *This better be good!*

"Hey, Yung-Su, a.k.a., Lil' Jay-Z! What's up?"

"I heard you moving to Georgia?"

"Let me guess, Justina told you too?"

"Yep! So when you moving, young girl?"

"Boy, who you think you calling young girl? You're the one named *Yung-Su*! And I don't know everything about the move yet 'cause my parents haven't been talking about it."

"Did you ask them?"

"I just told you they aren't saying nothing!"

"But, Lizzy, what happened to make you guys have to move in the first place?"

"Well, the short version is, as my daddy always says, my Aunty Faye moved out and left my grandma alone, and because she is older, she needs someone to be there for her. There is no one else to stay with her but *us*!"

"So why can't she move here?"

"That's what I said, Lil' J—I mean Yung-Su, ha-ha! But I am the kid, my parents make the rules, and I just try my best to follow. But can we talk later? My show is on."

"Sure, Lizzyyyy Babyyyyy."

"Whatever…boy!"

Finally, some alone time 'cause I sure do need it, I say to myself.

*****

Wow, it's morning! So no one woke me up? How long have I been asleep? I wonder. I don't smell any food, so it can't be the next day. Where is everyone? Wait, do I hear my Grandpa Charlie Mack downstairs or am I dreaming?

"Lizzy Baby, come down here. Your grandparents are here, and we didn't even know they were coming!"

Oh my goodness! I really need to see these two 'cause they do everything and anything to make me happy.

"Grandpa and Grandma Alexandra, I miss you guys, so much! You didn't even tell me you were coming home! I just talked to you on the phone, and here you both are!"

"We knew you needed us!" Grandpa says. "So here we are! We staying for two weeks, if that's ok with your parents."

"Sure is!" Dad says. "Your father knows he better say the right thing 'cause Charlie Mack don't take wooden nickels!"

"My mom is at work right now, and does she know you guys are here?" I ask.

"Nope, It's a surprise!"

Well, not anymore 'cause I hear the front door open and then a very loud scream. That's my mom screaming. She can't believe her eyes! It was complete shock for all of us; we never expected to see these two standing in the middle of the floor. What an awesome surprise, God, and thank you for letting my grandparents fly safely here. Yes! No matter what, today is a good day!

We go to Coney Island that evening, and what a wonderful, magical evening it is with my parents and my mom's parents who, mind you, flew in from Jamaica, all because they heard something in my voice. I am convinced that no matter what comes my way, I am blessed! Don't need nothing else to make me a believer.

My grandparents are older, but they love me enough to hop a plane and see about "Da Lil' Lizzy Gurl"—that's what they call me, Da' Lil' Lizzy Gurl. I think it's the funniest 'cause they are *so* serious! Their thick Jamaican accent makes it all the more meaningful and funny, I might add.

Once everything settles down for the evening, my mom and grandma are in the kitchen, I guess having girl talk. I decide that maybe it's "Lizzy wisdom time," and whatever that means, I strike up the convo with grandma.

"So, Grandma, what you think about us moving to Georgia? I mean, so suddenly, with such a short notice?"

"Excuse me, old young lady, *gurl*! Who in the Sam Hill ya talking to? Rest ya mind 'cause ya doin' too, too much rat now!"

"My mother needs to say no more 'cause apparently, I've crossed her line!" I tell her.

My grandma is even quiet, and when she shouts, her mouth…well then, I guess everyone should somehow be quiet!

"Lizzy baby, let us rest for now, and for sure, we pray on it, mon."

I am most certain it will work out—*it will work out*! Okay and good night are all I need to say for now!

*****

Boy oh boy, was my mom mad at me last night. I truly don't even want to think about it. Breakfast was great. My Grandma Alexandra made me the best blueberry pancakes I have ever had, and of course, my PaPa always has something to say like "Her panny cakes ain't no way better than mine!" My grandma just gave him the dirtiest look ever! Go, Grandma!

I need to get moving 'cause these fliers are not going to get themselves out there. After I, Justina, Malcolm, and Yung-Su hand out the fliers, it's back to visit Shoobie. Hopefully, we can act accordingly when we are in the hospital because we all certainly is about to be kicked out! It's funny now, but it wasn't then!

All hospitals have a funny smell, and sometimes I get very nauseous when I first walk in the door. But for some reason, that didn't happen today. Shoobie

29

is up watching his favorite cartoon, *SpongeBob SquarePants*, and he is really enjoying it 'cause I can hear him from down the hall. Wonder if he will get in trouble for being so loud.

"Hey, Shoobie, what's up? Your annoying butt getting any better?" I tell him.

"Be quiet, ugly Lizzy!"

"Ugly Lizzy—you the one in here with *two* casts on, so who's the ugly one, huh? I'll wait!"

"Now, now, that's enough!" my mom says.

My mom is still mad at me 'cause every time she looks my way, I feel something in my stomach. So yeah, I'm going to calm right on down before I have bigger problems than Shoobie.

I overhear the nurses saying that Shoobie will be home in one week, so I have got to get my father to take us to pick up his new bike. I leave the room to call my dad and ask him this big favor, and he didn't answer so I will remind him when I get home. He's probably out with PaPa having men time—whatever that may be. I bet PaPa talked my daddy into going fishing on the pier. My father loves to fish on the pier. He likes to catch those strips under the bridge. I will bet that's where they are.

Anyway, it's time to leave the hospital, we say our goodbyes, and we are on our way! Malcolm asked me to sit on my stoop and talk, so that's what we did, talking about our futures and what we need to accomplish in our lives. It was such a wonderful conversation 'cause I'm going to tell y'all one thing—Malcolm is super smart, so I know he is going to be successful! But I tell Malcolm that it's time to get cleaned up for dinner and that I will talk to him later. I watch him slowly walk down the street

Why he keep turning back around looking at me like that? I think.

Everyone was chattering it up at dinner, and I love to hear the stories and I listen to my parents and grandparents with so much love for one another. It lets me know where I get my good heart and spirit. God, did I thank you for the moments like this? 'Cause I really need to thank you!

My mom is not acting mad at me, probably 'cause she ain't thinking about no Lizzy baby. Right about now, she is enjoying her parents as she should! I watch my parents play a friendly game of spades and needless. To say my grandparents beat the seats off my parents is an understatement! When I tell y'all it's too funny, that's exactly what I mean!

*****

My father agrees that we all could go downtown to purchase Shoobie's new bike. He takes his big truck so that we all may fit in and plus the bike. It was a fun ride, and we just sang and laughed the whole way there! I love hip-hop, but you should see Yung-Su bouncing around in my daddy's truck. I don't know what else to say about that kid; he knows every word to Meek Mill's songs and don't get me started on Ice Cube or Drake! Heck, he likes them all! I do too, but he's really into it!

Whenever he hears about a show in New York, he hops on the phone, and one of his cousins is paid to chaperone him to and from the concert! My parents told me to *not* even think about asking them about some concert when I have plenty of time. In other words, they say I am not old enough yet! But yes, he is really going in on these songs. Me and Justina are back here cracking up and

Malcolm is in the front seat, which my dad planned it that way! But my father is really cool, and I think he understands what's up with me and Malcolm. But as his daughter, I know my dad. He is just waiting for the right opportunity to say something.

On the other hand, Ms. Afiya? Now she is not going to handle this well at all. So for all the young girls my age trying to have a crush on your neighborhood friend, think again 'cause the adults around my block—they on it! And that's a *good* thing. My parents say I'm going to college and I'm gonna make something of myself. Ain't no wasting *nothing* here! I got good parents, but dang! I can't have a secret crush on Malcolm in peace!

Fast forward to Saturday, and guess what? The streets are blocked off, and the cotton candy machine is up and running. The big "Welcome home, Shoobie" sign is flying high, all the neighbors have brought out their baked goods, and the clown is throwing his balls in the air and spinning his plates. The older people have lined up their chairs, and they all have a front-row seat. My father and Yung-Su's father have built a platform for me to present Shoobie his bike and to thank everyone, and today is going to be a good day! My grandparents are here from Jamaica, and they will get to meet everyone.

God, I don't ever remember being this excited in a very long time. I also have not forgotten the fact that my other grandma is alone right now as we all celebrate. So, God, with me saying all that, can you just fix what has been broken? In Jesus's name. Thanks again, Lord, for coming to rescue me.

Well, needless to say, all we hear are horns blowing from the other end of the block, and sirens are blurring, and kids are screaming, and guess what? It's Shoobie coming home with a parade of firefighters and policemen, and Justina and her parents are all riding together to bring him home. As they arrive in front of their house, everyone is crowding around the trucks, and we are all so excited! Everyone is out here, and my PaPa has put me on his shoulders so that I can actually see what's going on.

As they take Shoobie from the ambulance, I can see that he is so excited to be home, and the look on his friends' faces are priceless, not to mention the man who hit Shoobie is even here with his family 'cause when I share with you guys how scared he was when this all happened, I personally thought the man had a heart attack! But God has a mighty way of showing us things! Well, Franklin Street has seen the most of it. The end! For now, cause y'all know, we moving to Grandma Lizzy's house in Georgia!

About the Author

Waynette R. Cox has a bachelor's degree in science from Lincoln University, and she also has an associate's degree in arts from Eastern University. She served in the United States Army Reserve for eight years. Ms. Cox also enjoys reading and writing books and tending and caring for her garden, and she plans to one day travel the world and remind us all that we are not alone. She is the mother of two and grandmother of three.

This is the author's first children's book. All characters have been created for reading and learning the word of God through a younger generation. This is a fiction book, so no specific characters, places, or incidents are real.